Bibliographic information published by the German National Library:

The German National Library lists this publication in the National Bibliography; detailed bibliographic data are available on the Internet at http://dnb.dnb.de .

Imprint:

Copyright © 2017 GRIN Verlag
Print and binding: Books on Demand GmbH, Norderstedt Germany
ISBN: 9783668874008

This book at GRIN:

https://www.grin.com/document/455224

Nadiia Kudriashova

The Use of ERP in Practice. Benefits and Challenges

GRIN Verlag

GRIN - Your knowledge has value

Since its foundation in 1998, GRIN has specialized in publishing academic texts by students, college teachers and other academics as e-book and printed book. The website www.grin.com is an ideal platform for presenting term papers, final papers, scientific essays, dissertations and specialist books.

Visit us on the internet:

http://www.grin.com/

http://www.facebook.com/grincom

http://www.twitter.com/grin_com

The Use of ERP in Practice: Benefits and Challenges

Abstract

High competition is one of the main characteristics of the modern market. In order to ensure the competitiveness of its goods (works, services), it is necessary for the company to learn how to effectively manage all business processes, starting from the nomenclature of raw materials and ending with the control of financial flows and the formation of reporting. Creating a unified management system for all these processes is a task that ERP systems successfully solve. ERP systems SAP provide the customers with effective tools for accounting, planning, and management of all business processes occurring in the organization.

Increasing competitiveness is one of the main goals of implementing SAP ERP, for the implementation of which all functions of the system are directed. This goal can only be achieved by building a transparent and understandable business process management system based on complete and reliable information about the company's activities.

ERP systems have one more indisputable advantage, providing a stable development of the company - scalability. This allows maximizing the rational use of all their capabilities to support business growth and meet new challenges.

The purpose of the work is to analyze the key factors of the successful implementation of ERP-systems within the framework of the problem of interaction between management, employees of the company, and the external environment. In the course of the research, the following were conducted: analysis of the ERP system market, identification of the main trends, problems and prospects; highlighting the main advantages and disadvantages of implementing ERP-system in the enterprise; analysis of approaches to assessing the cost-effectiveness of implementing the ERP-system; generalization of ERP system implementation experience at specific enterprises, evaluation of implementation efficiency;

2

development of recommendations for replicating the ERP-system in accordance with the analysis.

As a result of the research, it was found that the implementation of ERP-systems is an expensive and resource-intensive process that distracts the management and production personnel of the company from the main activity for a long time. In this connection, studies of mechanisms for reducing these costs and overcoming resistance to change are relevant. The typification of the implementation of ERP-systems is expected to reduce the negative factors.

Contents

Introduction

The existing severe price competition in the economy and unstable macroeconomic conditions lead to the fact that in most sectors of the economy it is impossible to compensate for the consequences of excessive company costs arising from its unadjusted business processes by increasing the value of the products sold. As a consequence, one of the main tasks of management is to reduce the company's internal costs, primarily through the optimization of business processes.

The introduction of business applications is one of the main ways to improve the efficiency of the enterprise. This is the original purpose of corporate IT systems. Over the past 15-20 years, a large number of business applications appeared on the market, theoretically capable of solving most of the tasks facing the company. The most fully-featured business applications, including virtually all the company's required set of modules, are ERP (Enterprise Resource Planning system) -systems.

The implementation of the ERP-system is a complex technological process, which requires the enterprise to spend a lot of financial resources and staff time. At the same time, the implementation process involves a lot of internal and external factors that have a significant impact on the results of implementation, which results in a high probability of inconsistency of the final results of the implementation with the initial expectations. If it is not possible to use the implemented ERP system in the company due to the discrepancy between the realized functionality and the real needs of management and personnel, the enterprise not only loses the financial resources spent for implementation, but also faces the threat of a decrease in the efficiency of its work, due to arising of additional costs on the parallel implementation of activities in accordance with existing business processes at the enterprise and entering of information into an automated information system.

Therefore, the decision to implement the ERP system with a comprehensive assessment of the potential benefits of implementation is one of the key objectives of management when solving tasks to reduce the medium- and long-term costs of the company. This problem is especially acute when introducing complex, multifunctional systems that must solve not one specific task but provide solving a wide range of various tasks facing management.

As business, universities, and other enterprises become more vibrant, there is a constant need for these enterprises to seek new opportunities to enhance not just their productivity but also their competitiveness. This is critical in as far as meeting the demands of the consumers and end-users are concerned and enhancing the enterprises' agility. In terms of the enterprises' agility, this entails the following:

1) The response time of the enterprise to its direct and indirect consumers;

2) The quality of the products;

3) The efficiency in the enterprise's production and;

4) Overall production.

According to Davenport (1990, p.2), information technology is now being accepted and considered as one of the fundamental changes that enterprises must adopt in order to make sure that their agility is met. Albeit this suggested change in information technology, such change goes beyond switching from manual enterprises operational process to automated processes. With this comes the enterprise resource planning or the ERP system. In terms of information technology, applied in businesses and other enterprises, the ERP is considered to be one of the most advanced information systems that can augment the competitiveness of the business or enterprise.

Particularly, when adopted and applied properly to a business, will result to the acquisition of knowledge that pertains to organized management of the operations. It will also result in the ability of the businesses to provide its consumers with the right products or services at the right time with very low or with minimal cost. With this, one can simply adduced that the enterprise resource planning forms part of the backbone of a business. Hence, without it, the business can be exposed to the risk of failing. This is also the reason why huge corporations and even universities have incorporated and adopted the enterprise resource planning in their operations in order to ensure that their processes are integrated in a more effective and well-organized manner.

One of the most important innovations in enterprise resource planning system is the evolution of what is known as cloud computing. Over the years, cloud computing has resulted to the major changes how businesses and corporations use information technology to their advantage. With cloud computing, businesses have transformed the manner in which products and services are being paid for, devised, industrialized, deployed, measured, updated and preserved. The main purpose of cloud computing is to make sure that even with the integration of functionalities of information technology, the cost can somehow be managed effectively. This is because the upfront cost of the application of information technology and even the enterprise resource planning is burdensome to business owners. Bajwa et al predicted that by 2014, cloud computing will boom to become a $150 billion dollar business (2004, p.85). This prediction is not far off with the current standing of cloud computing because of the distribution of the system into three major models of service known as infrastructure, software business, and platforms. The use of cloud computing also adjusts to the needs of the consumers and businesses. There are options for public, private or the combination of both which is called hybrid cloud deployment (Coyne et al, 2016, p.154).

In terms of the enterprise resource planning system, on the other hand, researchers assert that the current application of the system on premise is not sufficient to meet the current demands and needs of e-businesses. Additionally, it is said that the intensive requirements needed for data and storage might cause for another innovation known as the ERP II or enterprise resource planning 2.0 (Gupta, 2009, p.337).

Basically, the enterprise resource planning system is not limited to what it offers to business owners of both huge corporations and small local businesses. It helps in most of the day-to-day business operations that owners can benefit from as productivity and efficiency increases. Its functionalities include but are not limited to:

1) Management of the business supply chain;

2) Automation of operations;

3) Efficient production and management of relationships between business and consumers, finances and accounting (Vaman, 2007, p.133).

The advantages of the enterprise resource planning system, when properly incorporated into a business or corporation can lead to vast opportunities for growth and expansion. However, it cannot be denied that there are also situations wherein the enterprise resource planning system poses risk and disadvantages to businesses. Hence, it is imperative that these advantages and disadvantages are studied in order to further understand how enterprise resource planning system can be appropriately applied in business and other enterprise.

In the traditional view, the evaluation of the feasibility of introducing an ERP-system is methodologically based on financial and investment analysis or approaches to project management and process analysis. At the same time, each of these methods is suitable for the analysis of only a part of the evaluation components of the feasibility of implementation. Methods of economic analysis are based on investment indicators that are difficult to be assessed prior to the implementation process and virtually any assessment embedded in the model for calculating investment indicators, initially based on empirical assessment of implementation risks, will ultimately be very different from reality and cannot accurately predict the return on investment in the ERP system. The methods of process analysis involve the evaluation of efficiency through the application of project management methods and monitoring of the duration of work and the level of their implementation, but they do not allow a pre-investment evaluation of efficiency and make a choice of the ERP system that best suits the tasks of the company.

Thus, proceeding from the increasing contribution of complex automation to the final result of the company's activities and the presence of tasks which are not solved by methods currently available for assessing the feasibility of implementing ERP systems, it becomes necessary to shape an integrated approach to the decision to implement an ERP system that includes both traditional financial and investment, as well as expertly evaluated quality parameters, which determines the relevance of the topic of this study.

Key Questions

In this regard, the aim of this paper is to identify the various advantages and disadvantages attached to the implementation of the enterprise resource planning software system to businesses and enterprises. Specifically, this paper will answer the following:

1) What are the advantages of the implementation of enterprise resource planning to a business?

2) What are the disadvantages of the implementation of enterprise resource planning to a business?

3) How can the identified disadvantages be mitigated or eradicated?

In accordance with the stated goal, the following tasks are assumed in the work:

- To analyze the current trends in the development of the market for the implementation of ERP-systems, the main methodological approaches to implementation and the difficulties that management faces when implementing a project for automating business processes;

- To investigate the basic functions and tasks solved by constructing a formalized development strategy (strategic vision);

- To analyze the role of a formalized strategy in deciding whether to implement ERP;

- To conduct an analysis of the main methods for assessing the effectiveness of implementation and operation of ERP-systems;

- To develop recommendations for the implementation of ERP-projects for the enterprises.

The practical importance of the work lies in the fact that the application of scientific and methodological developments and recommendations of the author allows increasing the organizational stability and efficiency of the process of implementing integrated management systems at enterprises.

Key Literature

There are many definitions of ERP-systems. One of them (the most frequently encountered recently) is the following: ERP-system is a set of integrated applications that allow creating an integrated information environment (IIE) for automation of planning, accounting, control, and analysis of all major business operations of the enterprise (Dillard & Yuthas 2006). It is generally accepted that IIE of the enterprises may include ERP-system; electronic document management software; information support for subject areas; communication software; collaborative software (tools to organize teamwork of employees); operational analysis of information and decision support; project management software; built-in tools and other products (for example, CAD/CAM/CAE/PDM systems, personnel management software, etc.). The basis of enterprise IIE is namely ERP systems (Laukkanen, Sarpola & Hallikainen 2007).

The impact of MRP/MRPII ERP systems on modern business cannot be overestimated. Already by the mid-1990s, the MRP/MRPII/ERP concept had become the main business model that manufacturers had used around the world to achieve production efficiency. For example, according to Advanced Manufacturing Research, by 1994 more than 48,000 of the 60,000 US industrial enterprises had operated these systems (Eden, Sedera & Tan, 2014).

ERP-systems have become so important for the operation of enterprises that, with any failures in their work, users have had considerable problems. For example, according to a survey of 886 IT managers of some of the world's leading companies (conducted by MERIT Project), their enterprises suffered the following losses due to forced downtime of ERP systems installed on them: from \$359,000 to \$1.07 million - 43.8%; from \$2.5 million to \$5 million - 35.3%; from \$9.3 million to \$10.7 million - 20.9% (Koh Gunasekaran & Goodman, 2011). The data obtained by AMR Research after studying 13 branches of American industry and 800 companies are also interesting. The purpose of the study was to find out which share of its budget the companies spend on ERP-systems. The results of the research are as follows: high-tech companies - 28%; pharmaceutical companies - 20%, financial companies - 15% (Coyne et al., 2016).

As analysis of the literature on the implementation and use of ERP-systems shows, the following main reasons can be singled out, as the result of which enterprises around the world are striving to introduce ERP systems (Behesti 2006; Haddara & Zach 2012; Tingting & Tortorella & Fries 2015; Ugrin 2009):

1. The main goal of implementing the ERP-system is the integration of all business processes of the enterprise under uniform rules and ensuring prompt receipt of information by management on all aspects of the enterprise's activities.

2. Ability to replace the set of derived stand-alone enterprise applications (for the most part obsolete) that do not meet the requirements of modern business, by one ERP-

system. For example, one well-known in the world oil producer, after implementing the ERP-system, stopped using about 350 derived applications.

3. Increasing the competitiveness of the enterprise.

Nevertheless, according to survey of the Worldwide Benchmark Project conducted among some of the world's leading companies, when using the MRPII/ERP system, it is more correct to speak of a reduction in corporate expenses rather than of real profit (82.5% of respondents when implementing the ERP system are monitoring costs and only 15% carry out observance of the growth of profits). However, more importantly, immediately after the deployment of the ERP-system, its indirect advantages begin to appear: the management of the enterprise has more time for comprehensive analysis and development of strategic decisions; closer relationships with customers and suppliers are developing; the burden on the administrative apparatus is reduced, etc. All this, in the end, leads to an increase in the efficiency of the entire enterprise (van Vuuren & Seymour 2013).

Successful companies always have room for growth and as they grow, departmentalizing would be their step towards an organized operation. It is important for companies to make sure that departmentalizing or separating functions into different divisions will not affect the efficiency of the company. This will be highly possible if there will be no communication barriers. For smaller companies, there may be tools they can use to solve this problem of expansion and division of work. However, larger companies need a more effective tool especially if they have a more complicated supply chain, larger number of suppliers and customers (Grant, 2003, p.99). These variables can make it hard for corporations to bridge the link between each department. However, because of enterprise resource planning or ERP, companies are successful with their aim in bridging information gap without affecting the operation's effectiveness.

If used correctly, ERP allows companies to tie the functions of each organization together where each department knows the events of the company in real time. It is highly beneficial for a company to have knowledge readily available to each department all across the entire organization. The implementation of ERP system offers efficiency and is one of the top ten benefits it can offer to an organization. The ERP system has various aspects that will make the operation process a lot easier and as a result, efficiency comes out naturally. Manual entry will also be lessened if not eliminated and thus, duplicate entry errors will be minimized too. This will also allow for the work process to speed up and work faster than the normal speed (Behesti, 2006, p.187). With the improvements and efficiency that the enterprise resource planning system has to offer, employees can in turn use their time and utilize their expertise in other ways for the benefit of the company. The act of improving the uniformity and availability of information creates a possible impact to the efficiency of the company operation process because it reduces the cycle time of the process (Grant, 2003, p.112). The improvements are the result of the software ability to standardize the processes among departments within the company. With the help of the system, each department has the ability to immediately respond in orders, which took them a substantial amount of time to complete with the previous process without the ERP system.

To understand the Enterprise Resource Planning or ERP better, the following scenario is a good thing to consider. Someone placed an order for a product with unique specifications. If the company does not have the enterprise resource planning system, there is a tendency that they will contact every department and suppliers in order to complete the parts needed to assemble the product. However, for a company with enterprise resource planning system, a few keystroke of the computer will do wonders including parts request, job order for workers, invoice creation, and even accounting entry.

With the given scenario, the job that took days or weeks with the company's previous process is done in minutes with ERP system. Another benefit that ERP offers to the company is the ability of the employees to make sound decisions on a daily basis as a response to the fast changes of their company. These benefits are accomplished in different ways. One way is the encoding of the data, that made easier and more automated, which resulted in a more accurate work. These data will now be the data available for use in all departments, available for collection daily without the need of a separation file or compilation making it readily available at all times. With the data and report available in seconds, executives enjoy the benefits of having reliable information that will support their decision when forced by the management to make decision within a short notice.

The use of ERP system also gives companies the ability to integrate technology because the software offers various integration options with e-commerce and supply chain partners. Considering the mentioned scenario above, the available technology that a company can integrate for the said scenario is to automatically place the customer's order on a concerned company's website. In a simultaneous manner, those suppliers with ERP system will get the message immediately, which is truly a great way to save time. After the order has been placed, all the concerned departments within the supply chain will get the updated status all because of the ERP system and web based collaboration systems. With the said modern process and collaboration, companies can now offer a service that is above and beyond what is expected, which is an advantage with today's fast paced society. Looking at all of the advantages mentioned, it is quite obvious that the main advantage companies enjoy with ERP is cost saving because it will lessen the time spent on a certain jobs. In fact, if the company would not want to utilize an employee's time, they can actually reduce manpower and save cost. With the efficient process, cycle times are already reduced and will result into more units produced. To have a better picture, we can take for example a simplified inventory process following order receipt will immediately show update to the inventory on hand thus will immediate reduce the inventory cost.

Also, the data provided will help the company in making sound decision for cost saving purposes. With enterprise resource planning system it would be easier to decide as to how much inventory to keep on hand because with the real-time update of inventory records, the company will have the idea and evaluate of its movement. With enterprise resource planning system, purchasing different software for different department will be eliminated and thus another cost saving benefit that companies will enjoy. This will also allow IT personnel to have a deep and effective analysis of the system because they will familiar only a single system, which will eventually saves their time and spend it into enhancing their knowledge of the enterprise resource planning system. With only one system, training cost will be minimized as well because employees can already introduce and train their new peers to the same enterprise resource planning system they are using (Fisher, 2006). Thinking of all the possibilities companies can do and the benefits they can enjoy, the enterprise resource planning system is truly an effective transformation tool for a company. Everyone in the organization from different departments can do their assigned tasks efficiently and in a timely manner. Fisher rightly claims that if the people in every department will not communicate, the company or organization as a whole will fail (Fisher, 2006). Because every department and its people have an important role in an organization, an effective way of communication is important and enterprise resource planning or ERP is the best tool for it.

However, as research shows (Maditinos, Chatzoudes & Tsairidis 2011, Muscatello & Chen 2008, Venkatraman & Fahd 2016), despite the undeniable advantages of ERP-systems, we should mention some problems that their users are currently facing.

Inefficiency of implementation. This problem is the main one and shows that any state-of-the-art technology will be useful only if it is correctly implemented and used. At many enterprises, which spent huge amounts of money for the acquisition and implementation of ERP-systems, their launch led only to negative results. It should be noted that according to analysts, up to 70% of ERP implementation projects fail (Venkatraman & Fahd 2016). In particular, the management of Hershey Foods, which spent $112 million to implement a comprehensive automation system, remained very dissatisfied with the significant deviation of the ERP-system implementation from the plan (the project included the supply of software, equipment, and services of SAP AG, Siebel Systems, Manugistics and IBM) (BCG 2016). At the same time, according to the Gartner Group, the compliance of the implementation projects with the planned indicators is estimated at 60% for ERP systems (of which "early implementations" is about 3%), and completely failed projects - at 10% (Haddara & Zach 2012). Other results of the BCG study also are quite indicative. A small number of successful implementations are noted. There is also no conclusive evidence that the enterprise benefits from the implementation of the ERP system. In addition, many respondents believe that the cost of implementing the ERP-system is too high (BCG 2016).

The complexity of effective integration of ERP-systems with third-party applications (primarily with e-business applications). If the previously created ERP systems were designed to integrate only the internal business processes of an enterprise (for example, passing orders or making payments), now more and more users want to combine their internal system (the so-called back office system) with an external frontend system, through which interaction with customers and partners is carried out. The main reason for respondents' dissatisfaction is the inability of ERP systems to successfully interact with e-commerce applications (Hanafizadeh & Ravasan 2011a).

Among the shortcomings also the low performance of ERP systems when integrating them with e-business applications (especially B2B) are noted, when it is necessary to quickly process simultaneous requests of many thousands of users about the status of their orders (Yongbeom, Zoonky & Gosain 2015).

The biggest disadvantage of an enterprise resource planning software system is the cost. Especially for small to medium sized businesses, the direct cost of the whole implementation process starting from exploration, preparation, testing, designing and customizing of an ERP can be very expensive. Aside from the financial cost, the training time spent for the employees and other stakeholders, and deployment of manpower should also be first considered by business owners if implementing an ERP system would be worth their time and money (Hardwood, 2003, p.36).

Since ERP is a generic system, business owners might opt to have their own customized system integrated in their current system, or build a new one. And since there are only a few experts in the field of ERP, it would take more time to train or employ an expert, than building their own. Like any other applications, web-based, offline or online software, a customized one can be very advantageous to a business, otherwise if not done correctly can do more damage than the business owners and corporations are prepared to (Hardwood, 2003, p.112). If business owners are opting to have their ERP to be customized, they should start aggressively from the planning phase. Entrepreneurs should also take into consideration the opportunity cost that will be spent on the adaptation of the new hardware to their company.

The usual pitfall of customization is the huge costing since an enterprise resource planning system project may take 1-3 years. This is why this is not applicable to small to medium sized businesses. Therefore, larger companies who have stretchable budget are more likely to customize their enterprise resource planning systems.

Customization of the enterprise resource planning system has various disadvantages. One of which is that it might be difficult to integrate with the other business processes and

17

operations when it is under customized. Secondly, the over customization of the same system might cause the production and operation to slow down. Finally, it could make it difficult for owners to upgrade the system (Huang et al, 2004, p.683).

Other disadvantages of the enterprise resource planning systems include but are not limited to:

Cost - Unlike if companies will just use those that are already available for free like Microsoft Excel or Access that comes upon purchase of the Microsoft Operating System, ERP charges companies accordingly. The charging is based on different factors making it an expensive investment for companies. Factors considered for ERP pricing are the number of users, application required, customization level and the hosting place. ERP cost is dependent on the number of users a company has. Therefore, larger companies will be charged more for they will surely have a larger number of users and they surely will require more applications for them to function effectively. Some companies also need a customized system especially those that are into specialized processes. Hosting can also be a huge factor for companies planning to use ERP system because they are to decide if they have it hosted in their own premises or in cloud storage.

Time Consuming – many of the companies claimed that they have no time for implementation because after a company decided to use the ERP system, the preparation will take 60 to 90 days or even more. If the company is a large institution, implementation of the ERP system could take years. Companies will have to undergo the process of going through the requirements making sure the software will perform and do its job and after the purchase has been done, the implementation process will immediately follow through including the evaluation and review, training and finally going live. While companies may use their in-house IT personnel for cost saving purposes, it is highly advised that they will seek assistance from an ERP expert, which will require time to complete because ERP implementation experts can only be counted by hands (Grant, 2003, p.99).

Training Required – it is important that in every department, there will be someone who are highly knowledgeable, otherwise, implementation would take longer. Therefore, an experienced user in every department is also important so that the implementation process will go on smoothly. In addition, while doing the training, every employee undergoing the ERP training will have to stop from working to focus in the training in order for them to have a better understanding of the system. This would only mean more pending jobs while training is on-going (Fisher, 2006).

Security Issues – many companies refused to use the ERP system because it will make them prone to information theft because ERP cannot protect companies from this type of security issue. Other than information theft, another security issue that a company can encounter if they chose to use the ERP system is the increased risk of misused information.

The choice of a specific ERP system for implementation is a complex and multi-criteria process due to the following main reasons (Hanafizadeh & Ravasan 2011b): the high cost of the purchased product (reaching several million dollars); a wide variety of ERP-systems offerings; the duration of training of specialists for the product being introduced, the pre-sales cycle (from several months to several years), and the implementation cycle itself (the ERP system implementation cycle can last up to several years even on one production site), as well as a number of other reasons.

In general, according to a fair observation of the researchers, when choosing an ERP system, one must understand that automation for the sake of automation does not make sense (Kim, Lee & Gosain 2005). It should be clear that the best ERP system in the world will not be able to solve all the problems of the enterprise. Any ERP system is, first of all, a tool for increasing the efficiency and quality of enterprise management, making the right strategic and tactical decisions based on automated processing of current and reliable information. At the same time, ERP-system is not only a tool for business but also a technology for its conducting.

Methodology and Data

The theoretical and methodological basis of the dissertation was made by the works of domestic and foreign scientists, as well as specialists and analysts in the following fields: information technology, assessment of the effectiveness of IT systems implementation, management and strategic planning, change management. For the processing of primary information, general scientific methods of analysis and synthesis were used. Methods of comparative, quantitative, and qualitative analysis, system analysis were applied, along with organizational methods of selecting and implementing ERP-systems.

This research paper will utilize the interview and qualitative data gathering method as it allows for a deeper comprehension of the behavior of the subjects of the research. It also allows for a fair interpretation of such behavior (Creswell, 2009, p.55). With the utilization of this method, the researcher will be asking broad questions as a part of data gathering which consists of impressions and opinions. This method will rely heavily on the ability of the author to provide correct and accurate interpretation of data to establish a clear answer to the questions posted. In addition, this research will benefit from the flexibility of the method as far as the presentation of additional questions is concerned; contextual factors; and the utilization of an appropriate theoretical framework (Creswell, 2009, p.55). With this type of research method, the researcher will be able to gather first-hand information and data pertaining and relevant to the topic of the research.

Also, open-ended questions will be used to gather direct and first-hand information from the participants in the study. In addition, second hand research will likewise be utilized in the completion of this paper. This means that the researcher will make an analysis and conclusion about the findings of the study based on the researches that have been published and written by other scholars. This type of research will utilize the information gathered from sources such as governmental reports, published journals, books, industry studies and other traditional forms of written works (Creswell, 2009, p.55).

The academic novelty of the research presented in dissertation is in the development and justification of the conceptual and methodological provisions that ensure the successful implementation of ERP-systems.

The distinctive feature of the results stated in the dissertation is the concept of a comprehensive assessment of the effectiveness of the ERP system integration as a means to improve the enterprise resource management system. In the author's opinion, the operation of the ERP-system is effective only in the case of a system solution of the management tasks set. If a decision is made to automate only one local task of the system (aimed at achieving a local optimum), then the ERP system in this case will be ineffective, since it will be an unnecessary burden, and not an instrument for increasing the effectiveness of management decisions.

Main features of the ERP system implementation market

Initially, the term ERP was applied to capacity utilization planning systems. Despite the fact that the term ERP arose in the production sphere, today it has a wider scope. Modern ERP-systems ensure the performance of all the basic functions of the enterprise, regardless of its type of activity or charter. Currently, ERP-systems are used both in commercial and non-commercial structures, in governmental and non-governmental organizations.

ERP-systems are often mistakenly called internal (back-office) systems, indicating that customers and the general public do not directly interact with them. They are opposed to external (front-office) systems such as customer relationship management systems with which customers work directly or e-business systems, such as e-commerce, e-government, e-telecom and electronic Finance (eFinance), and vendor management systems (SRM).

ERP-systems perform many functions in an enterprise scale. All functional divisions of the spheres of management or production are integrated into a single system. In addition to production, warehouse management, logistics and information technology, this system should include accounting, labor management, marketing, and strategic management.

Enterprise-wide software package (EAS) is a new name for once-developed ERP-systems, which include almost all business segments and use usual Internet browsers as thin clients.

The connection of the ERP system with OLAP technologies, the Balanced Score Card and the cost management system led to the emergence and development of BPM (Business Performance Management) systems - business performance management, which allow connecting the operational results of an enterprise with the effectiveness of the mission of the company. It is important what tasks do BPM systems solve and where do they rank among other software products for business process automation?

To answer this question, let us use the materials of the report "Best Practices in Business Performance Management: Business and Technical Strategies" prepared by the Data Warehousing Institute (DWI) 2014 (Yongbeom, Zoonky & Gosain 2015). This report positions BPM-systems, analyzing the general scheme of software development for business process automation for the last thirty years (Fig. 1).

First there were systems of automation of internal (back-office) processes, first of all production (inventory management and automation of production line management) and accounting. Then, at last, there was the turn of processes of interaction with the external environment (processes of the front office): supplies, sales, services, marketing. At the end of the twentieth century, organizations moved to automating cross-processes involving multiple

22

units, introducing customer relationship management (CRM), and supply chain management (SCM) technologies. And, finally, the top of the pyramid, which was automated recently, is corporate governance. To solve this problem, a special class of software is allocated in the world - the BPM-systems.

Software/IT

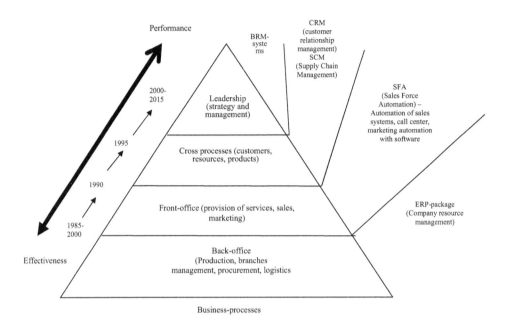

Fig. 1. BPM-systems.

Source: Yongbeom, K. Zoonky, L. & Gosain, S. 2015, 'Impediments to successful ERP implementation process,' Business Process Management Journal, No 11. Iss. 2. p. 160.

Moving up the pyramid levels reflects a gradual transition from automation of operational business processes to automation of business management strategy. Processes at higher levels of the pyramid control processes at lower levels. Thus, BPM-systems are designed to automate the strategic planning of business development and simultaneously to support tactical (or operational) management of business processes at different levels. The task of BPM-systems is to help in realizing strategic business goals in real conditions. To do this, they must provide the user with the right information at the right time to improve the management of operational activities (Yongbeom, Zoonky & Gosain 2015).

The functional architecture of the classical BPM system consists of three components. The first part is the data warehouse. This is the basis of the BPM system. It consolidates operational information from various automated modules of the head office and branches of the organization, from subsidiaries and partner companies. The second component is a set of tools to support enterprise management technologies: financial planning, management accounting, forecasting, management of production and support processes, etc. The third component of BPM is analytical OLAP tools for operational work with business data that are accumulated in the storage.

Thus, BPM-systems cannot be called something fundamentally new. They combine well-known management technologies and software solutions that were previously applied locally and solved the tasks of individual departments and users. What is the advantage and novelty of the BPM approach? The fact is that the BPM-system is designed to support the *full cycle* of company management. This means that BPM tools are interrelated and provide execution of four main stages of business performance management (Yongbeom, Zoonky & Gosain 2015, Eden, Sedera & Tan, 2014).

Strategy Development. The goal of the first stage is to identify business targets (key performance indicators) and to plan the quantitative values of their metrics (Key Performance Indicators (KPIs)). Strategic planning relies on one of the BPM methodologies, known as Balanced Scorecard (BSC).

Tactical planning. At the second stage, tactical plans are developed to achieve the strategic goals set. The guidelines for the development of tactical (operational) plans are KPI. The main tool for operational planning is the budgeting of various aspects of the enterprise activity.

Monitoring and control of execution. The third stage in the cycle of corporate governance is monitoring and control over the implementation of budget and production plans. The actual values for the items of management and financial accounting are calculated based on the primary data collected in the repository. To compare the planned and achieved budget and KPI indicators, the "plan-to-fact" analysis tools are used based on the multidimensional data analysis technology OLAP.

Analysis and regulation. At the final stage, strategic plans are adjusted in accordance with the actual operating conditions of the enterprise. To plan changes, tools are used to forecast and simulate various scenarios for the development of the situation. As a result, the cycle of corporate governance - between the chosen strategy and its practical implementation - is closed.

ERP-systems are focused on automation of management processes, maintenance of business processes and reduction of operating costs, but they are unable to provide comprehensive, easy and quick access to the necessary management information. In addition, it turned out that not all the information necessary for top management, as well as for managers and specialists in the field, is available in the ERP-system. This situation is exacerbated by the fact that often companies use not one but several ERP-systems, inherited as a result of mergers and acquisitions.

In contrast, BPM-systems provide a holistic, process-oriented approach to management decisions aimed at improving the company's ability to really assess its current state and manage the performance of its operations at all levels by uniting process owners, managers, personnel, and external counterparties within a common integrated management environment.

Let us note that in this sense, the concept of "BPM-system" can be used in two ways: as a management concept (i.e., a certain approach to the adoption of management decisions and their practical implementation) and as an information system (a set of software tools supporting the ideology of BPM and providing its practical implementation). This does not mean, however, that the BPM system "cancels" or "replaces" ERP. Figure 2 shows the possible interaction of ERP and BPM-systems (Muscatello & Chen 2008).

From the figure given below it is clear that the important role in the transformation of data from ERP- to the BPM-system is played by the so-called Data Maps modules - the means for unifying the data received from various sources and their alignment with unified directories (data conversion process). These tools are also used for feedback, for example, to transfer the results of strategic or operational planning to the ERP-system for the subsequent formation of more detailed plans.

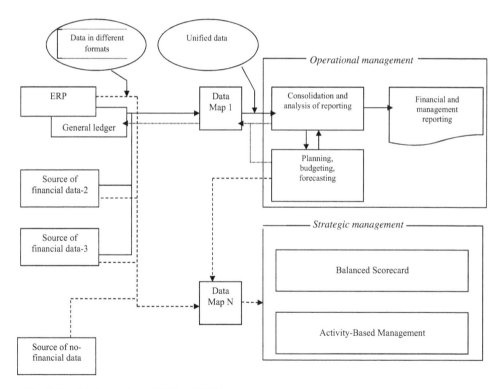

Fig. 2. Possible interaction of ERP and BPM-systems.

Source: Muscatello, J., & Chen, I. 2008, 'Enterprise Resource Planning (ERP) Implementations: Theory and Practice,' *International Journal of Enterprise Information Systems*, Vol.4, No. 1, p. 72.

Also, we should note that sources of financial and non-financial data for the BPM-system are not only ERP subsystems but also transactional systems of other systems:

• Customer Relationship Management (CRM);

• Supply Chain Management (SCM);

• Asset Management (AM);

• Human Resources Management (HRM);

• Other sources - databases, spreadsheets, etc.

Thus, using the "BPM + ERP" solution, an integrated infrastructure is created to support coordinated strategic and tactical management of the enterprise based on a single data model. This is the fundamental difference of the integrated approach based on the systems of automation of corporate management from an isolated solution of individual management tasks.

Priority number one for companies that initiate ERP projects is to improve business performance and performance indicators. This motivation for the implementation was announced by 17% of companies that launched projects in 2014. In general, for ERP business it is an opportunity to get significant effects - to improve qualitative and quantitative performance indicators, to integrate the information environment in a holding company that includes several companies for further development, etc. Many organizations are implementing ERP to replace existing ERP standard software that has 'have had their days' (33%), to replace software for automated accounting (22%), or as a modern alternative to 'self-written' control systems (20%). The remaining 25% are projects of the least optimized companies that implement ERP to replace "paper" management processes (Tingting & Yasuda 2016).

Analyzing the data of analytical studies of IDC, Gartner and TAdviser, it is possible to single out the following trends in the market for enterprise automation systems (Muscatello & Chen 2008, Tingting & Yasuda 2016, Venkatraman & Fahd 2016):

1. *Implementation of ERP to save businesses.* If in 2014, among the main reasons for automation of a production enterprise, entrepreneurs called improved control over operating profit, increased capitalization and compliance with the requirements of "transparency" in preparation for an IPO, today ERP is introduced primarily to improve the profitability of the business.

2. *The wave of transition to domestic software*, due to the adoption of the import substitution program.

3. *Cloud ERP solutions as one of the key points of market growth.* At the moment, enterprise management systems of this type are most popular among representatives of small and medium-sized businesses. Now, cloud ERP are applied to automate the simplest accounting functions. However, according to forecasts of Gartner, within 10 years this trend will become dominant, since cloud systems are cheaper and more convenient than stationary ones. In addition, this solution allows delegating part of the responsibility for maintaining the accounting activities of the company to a third-party franchisee (Tortorella & Fries 2015).

4. *Growth in demand for highly specialized solutions.* Typical automation systems are replaced by industry and individual automation systems. Increasing importance for enterprises is acquired by the flexibility of software products, creating the necessary conditions for their adaptation to the specifics of business processes and subsequent scaling. In addition, for the sake of economy, many are ordering vertically oriented solutions and individual highly specialized functional components such as EAM, HRM, and CRM.

5. Maintaining demand for mobile versions of ERP. The representatives of enterprises appreciated the convenience of monitoring and controlling production and business processes from improvised devices (phones, tablets).

6. Demand for 'boxed' ERP solutions from new projects in retail and manufacturing.

7. Using the ERP functionality for 30-50%. As a rule, at least 10 blocks are included in the complete set of modern automation systems for enterprises. However, to automate the key business processes of most enterprises, 3-5 modules appear sufficient.

According to the forecast of Allied Market Research (AMR), the world market of ERP-systems by 2020 will reach $41.69 billion, while the average annual growth rate during 2017-2020 will be about 7.2% (Allied Market Research official website).

In the global market, the SAP system continues to lead, with a share of 27% of the implementation of information management solutions in 2016, followed by solutions from Oracle (19% of the market) and Microsoft Dynamics (13%). Also popular are ERP solutions from Epicor and Infor (BCG 2016).

Most companies continue to implement "classical" ERP-projects and fully model business processes, configure and implement information systems. However, on the other hand, the number of such projects has decreased significantly: if in 2013 the percentage was 85, then in 2014 it was 56% (Bazhair & Sandhu 2015). That is, the number of companies that started using cloud management solutions (SaaS - software as a service) has grown rapidly (from 4% to 33%).

A significant increase in interest in cloud technologies in the context of ERP is not an unexpected phenomenon for the market, primarily because the market is very productively getting acquainted with SaaS solutions and their advantages, which include cutting IT costs, improving reliability, availability, scalability, and versatility.

Today, more and more organizations are moving away from on-premises-installations of ERP-systems towards solutions that are oriented to work in the cloud. Moving the local infrastructure to the cloud platform, the companies are getting more flexibility and mobility. However, the shift of outdated ERP systems is not always an easy task. In addition, companies that have spent hundreds of thousands, or even millions of dollars for local installation of ERP-services are unlikely to want to bother with the transition to the cloud in the near future. Instead of moving, it is easier to them to use a hybrid ERP model, where key services continue to work locally, and only part of the functionality is transferred to the cloud. The cloud approach is considered as an alternative to the hybrid model.

Cloud solutions have become a real trend since 2010. According to Kelton Research, about 68% of companies in the US somehow used cloud solutions. At this, solutions that are not the key ones were usually translated into the clouds, but today the activity on transferring ERP-systems to SaaS mode begins (Lenart 2011).

The approach in which services are entirely transferred to the cloud is interesting to the companies that are already using the cloud and want to improve services by adding additional functionality to them. Recently, companies prefer cloud-native ERP-solutions, as making changes to the functionality of this kind of service is much easier than working with local installations. The cloud model of ERP differs from hybrid and on-premise approaches. The fact is that in a hybrid model, when there is a cloud on one side and local installation on the other, making changes is not always easy, while cloud-to-cloud integration is simpler (Peng & Gala 2014, Coyne et al., 2016).

Companies with inherited on-premises-ERP systems, although they see the cloud as a flexible deployment tool, still find problems with managing large amounts of data, especially when it comes to the integration process. Despite these reservations, organizations still view the cloud as a means of improving business processes.

Production companies and organizations responsible for distribution are ideal candidates for using the hybrid ERP model. In addition, CRM, HR functionality and planning tools fit well into the cloud (Zhong & Rohde 2014). When it comes to e-commerce, e-payments, and collaboration, the cloud is capable of solving these problems.

The advantage of the hybrid model is in the ability to determine what to transfer to the cloud, and what to leave in the on-premises model. In this case, it is possible to transfer functionality entirely, which is best done in stages and sequentially. At the same time, if the ERP solution used is far from new, it does not support the service-oriented architecture, APIs, and other next generation-functionality, sooner or later it will have to be abandoned.

However, it should be noted that, like any cloud solution, ERP-system will operate in the same mode as the provider will determine, which does not always correspond to the needs of the company. Of course, companies are increasingly using hybrid systems, consisting of SaaS-solutions and modules of traditional systems, but the difficulties often arise with integration. Therefore, experts often emphasize not the lack of functionality in the deployment of ERP in the SaaS model but the increased risks of ensuring the continuity of business processes (Coyne et al., 2016).

In addition, each company in its own way builds processes and hones mechanisms. No matter how we try to approach some abstract ideal arrangement for business processes, because of industry, instrumental, human. and historical factors, there is no universal solution - each time the system needs to be adapted to a specific business. With own ERP-system, this adaptation is much easier than with a cloud solution.

Finally, it is believed that in the cloud environment it is still difficult to provide low-level monitoring of its operation, often associated with the control of the correctness of information usage and, as a consequence, creating the necessary logs, generating warning messages, processing events, etc. (Zhong & Rohde 2014).

While the cloud ERP solutions market is growing exponentially, most projects are still full-fledged implementations of corporate information solutions. According to the users themselves, the main reasons for this are a few: first of all, the lack of information on cloud products, the risk of a security breach, the risk of data loss (Coyne at al., 2016).

Still, cloud technology can be seen as the future of the ERP market. In addition, the main development factors are mobility of enterprise solutions and their availability on each device, exponential increase in data volumes and, as a result, built-in analytics (the Business Intelligence approach), increasing attention to the integration of everything that is possible in the enterprise with the corporate system, simplifying the configuration of ERP-packages and avoiding outsourcing support.

Development strategy and the role of ERP-systems in achieving the companies' goals.

Composition of the ERP-system

ERP class systems are an effective management tool for the enterprise, covering all the main business functions of the enterprise. So, with the successful implementation of ERP, an enterprise can gain a lot of significant competitive advantages, be it the optimization of production operations, the reduction of order processing time, better inventory management, or something else. However, all this is true only for cases of successful implementation. Unfortunately, ERP implementation projects often fail.

As criteria for selecting systems of the ERP class, the following are distinguished (Azevedo et al., 2012; Soja 2008; Ugrin 2009):

- Compliance with the current legislation and practice of interaction of enterprises in terms of necessary for the company full-fledged work with the external environment;

- Sufficient functionality of the system for the implementation of internal business processes of the company;

- Availability and completeness of means for customizing business processes;

- The possibility of changing the system for business development in the medium and short term;

- Simplicity of changes and modernization of functions for new business processes specific to the enterprise;

- Productivity;

- Ability to replicate to subsidiaries;

- The use of generally adopted, standardized IT technologies;

- The possibility of integration with other programs;

- Availability of opportunities that simplify the implementation process (for example, the learning environment);

- Coordinated work of various components and modules;

- Compatibility with the most common office programs;

- Availability of a standardized implementation procedure for all customers, which ensures guaranteed results;

- Timely software updates;

- The recommended implementation period;

- The number and qualifications of personnel required for the implementation team;

- Prevalence of specialists serving the system on the labor market;

- Providing technical support to users.

ERP-systems are designed to manage all financial and economic activities of the enterprise. They are used to provide the enterprise management with the information necessary for making managerial decisions, as well as for creating the infrastructure for electronic data interchange of the enterprise with suppliers and consumers. ERP-systems allow using one integrated program instead of several disparate ones. A single system can manage processing, logistics, distribution, stocks, delivery, invoicing, and accounting.

The system of delineation of access to information implemented in ERP is intended (in combination with other measures of information security of the enterprise) to counter both external threats (for example, industrial espionage) and internal (for example, data theft). Implemented in conjunction with quality control and customer relationship management systems, ERP-systems are aimed at maximum satisfaction of the needs of companies in business management tools.

In the typed ERP-systems, the following main functional blocks are implemented:

• Planning sales and production. The result of the block is the development of a plan for the production of the main types of products.

• Demand management. The block is designed to forecast future demand for products, determine the volume of orders that can be offered to the client at a particular time, determine the demand of distributors, demand within the enterprise, etc.

• Enlarged capacity planning. It is used to specify the production plans and determine the degree of their feasibility.

• The main production plan (production schedule). The products are determined in final units (products) with manufacturing terms and quantity.

• Planning of requirements in materials. The types of material resources (prefabricated units, finished units, purchased products, raw materials, semi-finished products, etc.) and the specific terms of their delivery for the implementation of the plan are determined.

• Product specification. It determines the composition of the final product, the material resources necessary for its manufacture, etc. In fact, the specification is the link between the basic production plan and the material requirements plan.

• Capacity planning. At this stage of planning, production capacities are defined in more detail than at previous levels.

• Routing / work centers. With the help of this block, both the production capacities of different levels and the routes in accordance with which the products are manufactured are specified.

• Inspection and adjustment of workshop plans for capacity.

• Management of purchases, stocks, sales.

• Financial management (general ledger management, settlements with debtors and creditors, fixed assets accounting, cash management, financial planning, etc.).

• Cost management (accounting for all enterprise costs and costing of finished products or services).

• Project/program management.

• Personnel Management.

In addition, for ERP-systems, the availability of electronic data interchange with other applications, as well as modeling of a number of situations related primarily to planning and forecasting, is practically mandatory.

In accordance with modern requirements, ERP-system must include the following modules in addition to the core that implements the MRPII standard (or its analog for continuous production):

• Distribution Resource Planning (DRP);

• Advanced planning and scheduling (Advanced Planning and Scheduling (APS);

• Customer Relationship Management (CRM, formerly known as Sales Force Automation);

• Electronic commerce;

• Product data management (PDM);

• Business Intelligence add-ins, including solutions based on OLAP technologies and DSS (Decision Support Systems);

• Stand-alone module responsible for system configuration (Standalone Configuration Engine - SCE);

• Final (detailed) resource planning for FRP (Finite Resource Planning).

Classic ERP-systems, in contrast to the so-called "boxed" software, belong to the category of "heavy" software products that require a fairly long adjustment, before beginning to use them. The choice of CIS, acquisition and implementation, as a rule, require careful planning in a long-term project with the participation of a partner company - supplier or consultant (Scheer & Habermann 2010).

Since the CISs are built on a modular basis, the customer often (at least at the early stage of such projects) acquires not a full range of modules but a limited set of them. During the implementation, the project team, as a rule, for several months carries out the configuration of the supplied modules.

Fig. 3 shows the relation of business size and type of integrated IS.

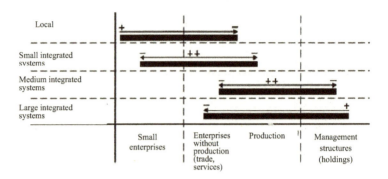

Enterprises

Fig. 3. The relationship between business size and the type of integrated IS.

Source: Developed by the author.

Choosing a ready solution is always a difficult and important task. The enterprise's intention to acquire and implement IS depends on many factors - from its internal readiness to re-engineer business processes to the price and time of IS implementation.

Ready solutions can be fairly divided into local, medium, and large integrated systems. Depending on the size of the business, the main goals of the tasks and the budget, the enterprise must determine for itself what solution it will be affordable and how much time can be planned for the implementation of the system.

If there is practically no problems with the acquisition of a small, usually "box" system, then with the average system - and even more so with a large one - everything is much more complicated. A large information ERP-system cannot be so easily bought, delivered, turned on and used. The enterprise should be thoroughly prepared for the implementation of such a system. The introduction of ERP-system is akin to a complex surgical operation - both here and there it is necessary to cut "live", and here and there a lot depends on thorough preparation, on the skill of professionals (Abugabah & Sanzogni 2010).

The choice of a specific ERP-system for implementation is a complex and multi-criteria process for the following main reasons:

• High cost of the purchased product (reaching several million dollars);

• A wide variety of ERP-systems;

• The duration of the training of specialists for the implemented product;

• Presale cycle (from several months to several years);

• the implementation cycle itself (the ERP system implementation cycle can last up to several years even on one production site of the enterprise).

In the right choice of ERP-system, the management of the enterprise should be primarily interested. The project to implement the ERP-system should be considered by the company's management as a strategic investment.

The main thing when choosing an ERP-system is to determine what new advantages will be given to the enterprise with its implementation. It is necessary to understand in detail what ERP-system can do for business, what objectives it can be realized and what impact it can have on the profitability of the enterprise and the cost of its products. At the same time, it must always be taken into account that the cost of delivery, implementation and maintenance of the ERP system cannot be more expensive than the cost of the entire business of the enterprise (Laukkanen, Sarpola & Hallikainen 2007).

First of all, the management of the enterprise must understand why the enterprise needs an ERP-system. Prior to implementation, clear and measurable targets set in the so-called S.M.A.R.T system should be set: the goals must be specific, measurable, adjusted, relevant and have a certain time of execution. It is desirable that the answer to this question can be formalized and presented graphically in figures and diagrams (volume of savings, higher turnover of goods, shorter time for work with suppliers and customers, etc.). The main requirements for the ERP system must be formulated and approved by the company's management:

• What goals of economic activity and tasks of business as a whole will be implemented due to the acquired and introduced system;

• What functional areas and types of production should it cover;

• Which processes should be automated;

• What reports should be prepared;

• What software and hardware platforms should be used.

It is very important to clearly define the current and future needs of the enterprise or organization. It is necessary to understand well what drives the business, what factors are critical for success and what is necessary for the company's development. The requirements cab be in the form of a special document (Vision Scope), in which all desirable characteristics of the ERP system are identified and prioritized.

It is equally important to correctly assess the existing technological infrastructure of the enterprise. If for an ERP system implementation an enterprise first has to spend significant funds (comparable to the cost of the implemented system) for the modernization of its local or global networks, this option may not be profitable. Generally, the implemented ERP-system must correspond to the existing financial and technological levels of the enterprise.

It should also be understood that the greatest effect is achieved with the integrated implementation of ERP-system. It makes no sense to spend huge sums to buy a system, the capabilities of which will not be used in full, or a system that will need to be constantly completed.

An extremely important point is the correct choice of the developer (or developer-implementer) of the ERP-system, which should not only deliver its software to the client company but become its long-term partner providing support and further development of the system.

The client enterprise must be confident in the high quality and timeliness of future upgrades of the installed ERP system (when new versions appear), in solving all problems related to its flexibility and scalability. If the implementation is carried out by a consulting company, it is equally important to understand the relationship between it and the developer of the ERP system. In any case, it is very useful to arrange a tender between suppliers. The organization of the tender will significantly reduce the initial price of supply and allow better understanding the possibilities – of both the proposed systems and their developers.

The implementation of the ERP-system should be carried out by the development company (or, in some cases, by the developer company) with the closest contact with the IT department and the relevant interested departments of the enterprise. After the implementation of the ERP-system, certain types of modernization work can be entrusted to external consultants of the company-developer (consulting firm), and its general support can be left for the IT department.

It is not just a set of programs with documentation that is purchased (most of which are developed on standard tools and are based on common platforms) - the work and experience of the shaped team of an ERP system developer are acquired, bearing various types of responsibility (from legal to moral) for quality and efficiency of the installed and maintained software and technological systems.

In some cases, enterprises focus on the systems developed by their own IT departments. Practice shows that orientation to "self-written" systems allows getting the IS, most suitable for the company's business, but ultimately puts the company in dependence on its own developers. Rarely, such an independently developed software product remains viable for quite a long time, as there is usually no corresponding complete and up-to-date documentation on it. It cannot be said that it is professionally tested at the stages of development and commissioning and is reliably supported. A large enterprise can afford to invest in the development of its own (under its specific needs) CIS only if the following basic conditions are met:

• There is no ready-made software product on the market that satisfies the enterprise in terms of functionality, cost, and maintenance conditions;

• The enterprise has a powerful IT department with experienced analysts, project managers, and programmers;

• There is a complete and competent statement of the problem;

• There is a technical possibility to simulate the work of the created software during the trial operation;

• There is a possibility of real support of the created system by own forces;

• There is an ability to replicate developed software for subsidiaries (industry) enterprises.

The main problems of implementation and use of ERP-systems

Despite the indisputable merits of ERP-systems, we should note some problems that their users are currently facing.

In the report of Boston Consulting Group, the problem of enterprise satisfaction with the results of implementing ERP-systems was investigated. In the course of the research, 100 IT managers responsible for implementing the enterprise ERP system during the last 5 years were surveyed. According to the analysts of BCG, ERP-systems are vital for enterprises but the success of implementation depends on whether they were able to adapt as closely as possible to the business processes of the enterprise or, conversely, to rebuild business processes for standard functionality of the ERP system (BCG 2016).

In frames of our research, we conducted a survey of 50 companies that implemented the ERP-system. It was revealed that organizational elements of different levels of management and specializations participate in the system integration process, which makes it more difficult for effective interaction at all stages of integration.

The survey results show that only one third of the enterprises are satisfied with the results of implementing the ERP-system when evaluating the pricing criteria, price effectiveness, real financial impact and achievement of the set goals. About 50% of users of ERP-systems evaluate their financial, production and personnel applications as inadequate to the goals set (only about 30% estimate the implementation of the ERP-system as successful).

Other results of the study are also quite indicative. There are relatively few successful implementations.. While 60% of managers believe that their efforts to implement such systems have brought significant benefits, 52% believe that they have achieved their business goals, and only 37% note a noticeable positive financial effect after the implementation of the ERP system.

In the course of the survey, the customers' dissatisfaction with the developers of ERP-systems was also revealed. 15% believe that ERP developers do not focus on business objectives, 33% believe that ERP developers only contribute to unjustified expenses of their customers, and 12% simply terminated the contract with their first ERP-supplier. In addition, many respondents believe that the cost of implementing an ERP-system is too high. Every fifth implementer at the ERP-system believes that he could do the same for a lower price (they also believe that more than half of the expenses were superfluous). All interviewed managers consider ERP-systems of lower cost the best.

As a result of the research it was found that the implementation of ERP-systems is an expensive and resource-intensive process that distracts the management and production personnel of the company from the main activity for a long time. In this connection, studies of mechanisms for reducing these costs are relevant. Typification of the implementation of ERP-systems will reduce the negative factors.

Experience shows that the average cost of projects for the implementation of ERP-systems that received a positive assessment is 7-10 million dollars, and the average cost of the project with a negative rating is up to 90 million (Yongbeom, Zoonky & Gosain 2015).

According to the research of Gartner Group, in many cases, successfully implemented system does not fully realize its functions due to unsatisfactory use and maintenance. There are many reasons for this: insufficient preparedness of the enterprise, poorly trained personnel, lack of a security policy, obsolete network and electrical equipment, etc. (Fig. 4) (Haddara & Zach 2012).

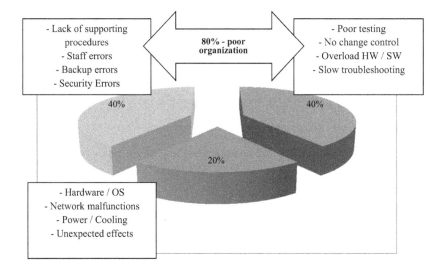

Fig. 4. The main reasons for the downtime of CIS (according to Gartner Group).

Source: Haddara, M. & Zach, O. 2012, 'ERP systems in SMEs: An extended literature review,' *Int. J. Inf. Sci.*, 2, pp. 110.

The quality of the project of ERP-system implementation also does not always satisfy the customer. At 58% with a positive assessment of the results of ERP-system implementation, project executors completed them on time and within the budget. A similar picture is typical for 33% of respondents with a negative attitude towards the results of the ERP system implementation.

There are also data from the Standish Group that only in 16% of cases the full-scale implementation of ERP-systems ends on time and within the planned budget. Almost in 30% of the cases, the implementation is terminated early, in other cases, the timing/budget of the implementation project is exceeded or the functionality specified in the project is limited. In connection with all of the above, suppliers of ERP-systems prefer to talk more about their

45

experience of "productive," rather than "successful" implementations (Soliman & Karia 2016).

Speaking about the complexity of effective integration of ERP-systems with third-party applications, first of all we should say that this applies to e-business applications. As it was mentioned above, if previously created ERP-systems were designed to integrate a large part of the internal business processes of an enterprise (for example, warehouse management, order management or payments), now more and more users want to combine their internal system (Back-Office) with External system (Front-End), through which the interaction with customers and partners is carried out.

The main reason for the dissatisfaction of managers is the inability of ERP-systems to successfully interact with e-commerce applications. The fact that it is difficult to link ERP-systems with e-commerce applications is also evidenced by the results of AMR Research. Of the 800 companies surveyed, only 15% provide their customers and partners with the ability to check the status of the order directly on the Web site, and only 5 to 10% allow them to carry out transactions. According to various estimates, at present there are not many e-shops where full integration with server systems is established. In some online stores, an order received via the Internet is still sent to the employee who manually enters it into the ERP system (Venkatraman & Fahd 2016).

It should be also noted limited analytical capabilities of ERP-systems and insufficient support for decision-making processes. ERP-systems are good at obtaining and storing data; when it comes to analyzing and processing information, the possibilities of ERP-systems are very limited. The data scheme used to manage enterprise resources is very complex. All corporate data are "inside" the ERP-system, but they remain "hidden", and extraction of them for analysis is quite difficult. In addition, ERP-systems are not fully integrated with other applications and external sources of information, where data is received for analytical processing.

For example, PacifiCorp (part of the ScottishPower group, with 8,000 employees), which supplies electricity to 1.4 million consumers (home, commercial, and industrial) in 6 Western US states, has implemented the ERP system SAP R/3. After PacifiCorp integrated its inherited systems into the SAP R/3 environment, it turned out that critical business information needed to analyze the state of stocks, personnel, finances, customers, etc. became inaccessible. In fact, after the introduction of R/3, the ability to quickly access this information was seriously hampered. PacifiCorp had to implement additional PowerConnect for SAP R/3 software and PowerCenter software (developed by Informatica) to provide access to this information and integrate it with information stored in the customer service system (Eden, Sedera & Tan 2014).

Evaluation of the effectiveness of the implementation of ERP-systems

Theoretically, ERP-system, introduced into commercial operation, should become a source of full, timely, and reliable information on all economic aspects of the enterprise activity, a means of optimizing all expenses and incomes of the enterprise at all levels of management, as well as a tool for conducting corporate policy and compliance with the corporate economic strategy. As a result of using such a system, the economic level, it will be possible to "brought to" what cannot be optimized at the technological level (on which specific products and processes of their production are considered), which will maximize the return on the enterprise activity.

Among the main results, users note the following: accessibility of information, increased interaction opportunities; increasing the integration of business processes; timeliness, relevance, and reliability of data; increasing productivity and efficiency; improved customer interactions.

Quantitative evaluation of the cost-effectiveness of implementing ERP-systems causes significant difficulties, since there are no reliable methods for calculating the values of the above indicators in practical terms. The issue of introducing a modern management system is equivalent to the issue of enterprise survival (Law & Ngai 2007). Without the presence of such a system, the enterprise simply turns out to be outside the general economic processes. The effect of the project implementation of the ERP-system is also difficult to be assessed directly in the money. The difficulties in calculating the economic effect from the implementation of ERP-systems are aggravated also by the fact that in real life far from everything can be formalized and entered into the ERP framework, that is why part of management processes, staff motivation, production, etc. remains outside the single information system.

The effectiveness of the introduction of the corporate information system should be evaluated by the return on investment (return on the cost of investment). In the general case, the following indicators are taken into account (Fig. 5) (Hanafizadeh & Ravasan 2011b).

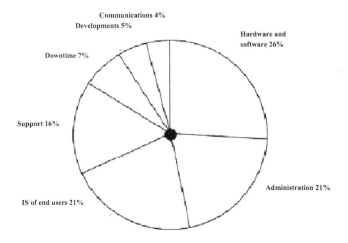

Fig. 5. An approximate composition of the total cost of ownership of IS (ERP).

Source: Developed by the author based on the analysis of data.

In fact, this is Total Cost of Ownership (TCO), which includes software, hardware, the cost of external services and costs of operation, maintenance and salaries of specialists and staff. Figre 5 shows an approximate composition of the total cost of ownership.

Meta Group company conducted a special study of the cost of ownership of the ERP-system (TCO), which included hardware and software, as well as the cost of services and staff costs. The final amount included costs for installing the system and a two-year implementation period during which the system is maintained, updated or enhanced and optimized. Among the 63 companies that participated in the study (they represented different industries and were classified as small or medium and large businesses), the average value of TCO was $1.5 million (ranging from $400,000 to $3 million). There are also estimates by foreign analysts that the cost-effectiveness ratio when implementing MRP/ERP systems is in the range 0.25-2.0 (van Vuuren & Seymour 2013).

The time to implement (TTI) is also important, in addition to which it is necessary to take into account the time it took to pay back the implementation (the total time is called Time to Benefit - TTB).

Return on investment (ROI) is another indicator. According to the Meta Group research, the average ROI after the introduction of ERP-systems was $1.6 million per year.

The total cost of the enterprise for the implementation of the ERP-system (Net Present Value - NPV) includes the costs of software and hardware, services, wages, post-implementation costs. and return on investment.

In the implementation project (at all its stages) the employees of the enterprise must necessarily participate to accumulate experience for the subsequent maintenance of the system. At the same time, the level of qualifications and abilities of the employees involved will directly influence the success of the entire implementation project. The more serious the attitude of the management towards the selection of personnel for the implementation group, the more the company will benefit from the introduction. The specialists of the enterprise, members of the implementation group, must necessarily receive training (the cost of which for ERP-systems can reach hundreds of thousands of dollars).

When organizing the implementation of the project, it is necessary to clearly separate the consulting support for the ERP system implementation and the direct implementation of the ERP system. Under the consulting support of the implementation the training and consultations of the employees of the enterprise on various issues is understood (setting up the modules, the peculiarities of their use for solving specific problems at the stage of survey and implementation, etc.). Consulting support is carried out by specialists-implementers. In turn, the employees of the enterprise that are members of the implementation group should be engaged in direct implementation (forming the base of normative and reference information, modeling the processes of activity, conducting the experimental operation of the ERP system and putting it into commercial operation).

Practical steps to introduce CIS are shown on the Fig.6.

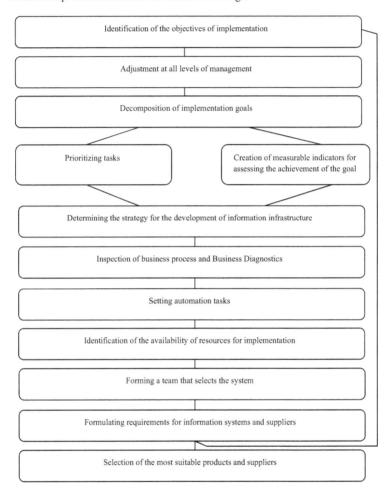

Fig. 6. Practical steps to introduce CIS (ERP).

Source: Developed by the author.

In the process of implementation, the enterprise should receive not only an adjusted and functioning ERP-system but also its own professionally trained employees, capable of independently supporting it (an important point is also the additional material and moral incentives for the employees of the enterprise participating in the implementation project).

The implementation of the ERP-system is always accompanied by a certain adjustment (optimization) of both the organizational and staff structure of the enterprise and the processes of its operation. At the same time, the main criterion for the necessity of changes is their expediency from the point of view of ensuring the efficiency of the enterprise management process as a whole.

The management of the enterprise should understand what these changes will lead to, and (after making a decision about the changes) consistently implement them. Summarizing the above, it is possible to formulate a list of the most important practical steps for the initial phase of the introduction of CIS (Fig. 6).

With the right, carefully planned implementation, companies can achieve really meaningful results, such as the following (Azevedo et al., 2012):

• Decrease in operating and management costs 15%;

• Savings of working capital 2%;

• Reduction of the sales cycle by 25%;

• Decrease in commercial costs of 35%;

• Reduction of the insurance level of warehouse stocks 0%;

• Decrease in accounts receivable 2%;

• Increase in the turnover of funds in the calculation of 5%;

• Increase in inventory turnover of 30%;

• Improvement of the utilization of fixed assets by 30%.

Development of recommendations based on the analysis of projects for the implementation of ERP-systems in enterprises

The goals and requirements set by the enterprise management for the ERP system implementation project are determined by the company's development strategy, key business objectives. The largest players in the market of ERP-systems offer corporate solutions that allow for flexible configuration of the functionality of the system. In some cases, the objectives of the implementation project are set based on the specific capabilities of the information system, which was chosen as optimal for implementation at a particular enterprise.

Currently, the practice of implementing projects to implement ERP-systems for enterprise management is a very complex and risky activity. There are various estimates of the degree of success of completed projects and their real economic efficiency, but they all agree that the number of projects that meet the criteria for success and meet initial expectations is very small. The reasons for the failure or partial failure of most projects to implement ERP-systems are very similar, despite the specificity of the subject area in each individual case of implementation. Errors of implementation and/or preparation for the implementation project can be classified according to the following characteristics.

Problems related to the internal state of the enterprise

1. The principles of company management (business management) are partially or completely not formalized or even chaotic. Internal business processes are not obvious and not unambiguous.

Before embarking on the implementation of the automation system, the enterprise needs to perform a partial (determined depending on the real need) reorganization of the main processes that provide the solution of business problems. Therefore, one of the most important stages of the implementation project is a complete and reliable survey of the enterprise in all aspects of its activities. Based on the results of the survey, the whole further scheme for building a corporate information system is being built. Undoubtedly, one can automate everything on a "as-is" basis, but this should not be done for a number of reasons. As a result of the survey, it is possible to identify a significant number of unreasonable costs, as well as inconsistencies in the organizational structure and processes, the elimination of which will reduce production costs, and significantly reduce the execution time of the various stages of the main business processes.

2. Resistance of employees of the company involved in the project, to the implementation process. When implementing corporate information systems, in most cases there is active resistance of employees in the field, which is a serious (and perhaps most significant) obstacle for the consultants of the executing company and it is quite capable of frustrating or significantly dragging out the implementation project. This is due to several human factors: the usual fear of innovation, conservatism, the fear of losing a job or losing one's indispensability, the fear of significantly increasing responsibility for one's actions, the unwillingness to carry out additional work related to participation in the project. The managers of the enterprise, who decided to automate their business, in such cases should in every way promote the responsible group of specialists implementing the information system, conduct explanatory work with the staff, including:

- To form a firm conviction among the company's employees of the necessity and inevitability of implementation;

- To inform staff regularly about the status and progress of the implementation of the project;

- To identify the instigator of resistance, find an individual approach to him, neutralize his efforts for sabotage or as a radical way – to fire him.

Errors in preparation for the implementation project

1. The main objectives of the project have not been defined, criteria for achieving the objectives and evaluating the results of the project have not been approved.

The clearly stated goal of the project is one of the main necessary conditions for the beginning of the entire implementation project. Namely because of the uncertainty of the objectives of the implementation or even the absence of such, a significant number of implementation projects ended in failure or an uncertain outcome. The objectives of the project should be fixed in quantitative and financial terms. A typical error of the management is to start the project with the only desire to start the project, and evaluate the results as soon as it moves. Analysis of even very successful implementations at first glance shows that they took place within four to five years. This means that automation was performed cyclically. The project will be endless and absorbing more and more resources until the concrete clear objectives of the project are fixed and the concept of their achievement is formulated.

2. Incomplete, inaccurate or changing requirements for the system.

3. Designing requirements for the system by the principle "bottom-up."

Laying in the ERP-system of the company's goals and prospects for its development can only be done in a top-down design, and not vice versa. Each level of management has its own information support needs. The distribution of information flows will be correct if to start building the system with the specification of the needs in the information of the upper levels of management, gradually going down. With this approach, first of all, the indicators required by the top management are formed and determined, as well as the frequency of their calculation. Then, the data required for the next management unit in the hierarchy is set, etc. Thus, the risk of creating a system that will generate information insufficient to make managerial decisions by top management is excluded.

In practice, designers not aiming to provide information support for making management decisions, try to enter the maximum amount of data into the system, thus unreasonably increasing the cost of automated control systems, or they lose some of the information important for some level of management. As a result, management suffers because of the inadequacy and untimeliness of obtaining the necessary information.

4. Designing without taking into account the company's development strategy.

This is one of the typical mistakes in preparing for the implementation of the system. The projected system is designed to automate the management of the company in its present "form," that is, without taking into account its future development. The system needs to be designed so that it will work for 2-3 years without modernization. Therefore, when designing, it is important to represent the structure and scale of business in the long term for at least 3 years. Errors in forecasting can lead to unreasonably high costs, in particular for the purchase of additional network equipment and Internet traffic, which account for a significant share in the cost of ownership of the ERP system.

Possible directions of the enterprise development or changes in its activity can be the following: technological changes in production; creation of a branch network; replacement of suppliers; reduction of reserve stocks, etc.

5. Initiative implementation comes from the IT-service or from the shareholders of the company-customer, rather than from the direct management of the company.

The practice of successful projects in the implementation of information systems shows that the purpose of implementation is more likely to be achieved when the initiative for the acquisition and implementation of the system comes from the direct management of the company, which is competent in the subject area and specific production activities of the company. Often, the information service (information department) or the shareholders are proposing to introduce a new automated management system in the company. At the same time, the goal set for the implementation project is far from the true interests of the company. The IT service may be interested in getting new hardware into its "possession" (which is most likely to be done as part of the system implementation project), and the company's shareholders in their effort to get a new management system are only trying to improve the rating and the company's credibility for the future increase value of shares of companies. This does not take into account the real need to update the software used in the enterprise.

6. A qualified group for the implementation and maintenance of the system has not been formed, a strong team leader has not been determined.

Most major automation systems are implemented using the following technology: a small (3-6 person) working group is formed at the enterprise, which passes the fullest training in working with the system, then a significant part of the work on the implementation of the system and its further support falls on this group. The use of such a technology is caused by two factors: firstly, by the fact that the enterprise is usually interested in having at its fingertips specialists who can quickly solve most operational issues while setting up and operating the system, and secondly, training their employees and their use is always significantly cheaper than outsourcing. Thus, the formation of a strong working group is the key to the successful implementation of the implementation project.

A particularly important issue is the choice of the head of such a group and the administrator of the system. The manager, in addition to the knowledge of basic computer technologies, must have a deep knowledge of business and management. In practice, when implementing systems, this role, as a rule, is played by the head of the ACS department.

7. There are no project implementation milestones for the implementation of the system.

The project is not divided into controllable blocks, control points have not been allocated, and as a result, the project implementation deadlines are delayed. The following recommendations can be proposed:

- To identify the directions that need to be monitored; to appoint responsible persons for each of them (for example, for technical facilities and infrastructure, training of end users, organizational changes, software development, optimization of business processes, etc.);

- To select the functional blocks of the future system, establish the order of implementation of the program modules, and fix the project control points.

8. Excessive change of business processes "for" implementation; adjusting the company's internal processes to the capabilities or requirements of the system, and not vice versa.

Quite often, a company implementing ERP-system either agrees to re-engineer all business processes and their subordination to the requirements of the basic functionality of the chosen system, or insists on maintaining the established practice of work and, accordingly, on the cardinal reorganization of the chosen system (and sometimes even on its full rewriting). In the first case, there is a great risk that the system created based on the cardinal reorganization of business processes will not be used at all. In the second case, the resulting system, due to modifications and rework, loses its reliability.

9. The management of the company incorrectly estimates the potential economic effect of the result of the future implementation of the CIS, which can mean the failure of the project in terms of payback. A successful project can be called in the event that the final indicators coincide with the planned at least 70-80% (Aladwani 2011). Side-effects (overdue dates and spent extra-budgetary money) take place very often.

The introduction implies considerable costs for general automation (computers, servers, network equipment, licenses, consulting services, etc.). In this regard, it is important to compare the costs of automation of a process, taking into account its place in the ERP-system, with the final economic results of the project as a whole. That is, it is necessary to answer the question: what will allow keeping records of corresponding operations in the system or providing specific data to a definite manager? What losses will it help to avoid?

Answering the question, what is the price of inclusion of any information, is necessary at all stages of ERP-system design. First, when determining its functional structure, choosing the basic platform, technical support and other general solutions for the system at the stage of developing its concept; then when drafting a technical assignment. In addition, the question of economic efficiency is important at the design stage of the system, and not on the eve of commissioning.

It should be noted also the problems that arise directly in the implementation.

1. Training of personnel is not organized during and after the implementation of the project.

One of the indicators of project success is the "alienability" of it from outside consultants. It's about how easy every employee of the company from the CEO to the assistant manager after formal completion of the project will be able to cope with the system without help from outside. Therefore, competent managers include an instructor-teacher in the project team. He trains users for a future solution to the new functionality. It is very useful if the teacher not only formally refers to his duties, but also purposefully forms in his listeners a positive perception of the implemented system, or, in other words, "manages expectations."

2. Implementation is made only by external consultants. Employees of the company-customer do not participate in the project implementation.

As a rule, the management of the company implementing the ERP-system believes that after the implementation by the project consultants, the expected result will be achieved. However, this opinion is erroneous, since the company's employees cannot always clearly articulate and communicate their vision of the project results to the specialists in the implementation. Often, employees of the company implementing the ERP-system perceive consultants on implementation as "good wizards" who, after listening to all the wishes and expectations, will do everything properly. This will not happen only through the work of consultants. In a full-fledged project implementation team there are specialists with various functional responsibilities, including employees of the customer company.

3. The project team does not have sufficient authority for active implementation. The project itself does not have an official top priority for the company's management. The management of the customer company needs to set a high priority for the project implementation of the system among all other organizational and commercial services within the company, give high authority to the project manager, allocate the necessary resources (the employees and their time in this case) to conduct the implementation work. Only in this case, the implementation project will not be "overwhelmed" under the current activities of the company and will have a chance of successful completion.

ERP-system of the enterprise is a fairly developed system, and its functions are in a constant stage of development and improvement, but still, it happens that after the ERP-system was implemented at a certain enterprise and all methods of its implementation were properly used, the enterprise management still cannot get full information control over the activities of the enterprise. Among the experts, there is an opinion that the projects of implementation of automated control systems do not give positive results due to the fact that when designing these systems the business development strategy is not taken into account, too often reprogramming of business processes is carried out.

It often happens that a company that decided to implement an ERP system is taking such a significant step as re-designing or reengineering all existing business processes at the enterprise and further implementing them and obeying the requirements of the ERP system.

When reengineering all business processes, the risk increases that the ERP system implemented at the enterprise will not be used at all.

Preservation of all existing business processes is also an inefficient method, because the resulting system, due to multiple modifications and processing, loses its reliability and effectiveness. This affects the risk of erroneous processing of input information, and automation of the chosen system will also not be of any use, since the processed and revised business processes will be ineffective. The enterprise in this case will depend on the chosen management system and will automatically lose the opportunity to improve its activities. On the basis of these methods, it is important to find a golden mean between business process reengineering and finalizing the existing system.

It should be emphasized that the problem of implementing ERP-systems lies more in the organization of the project itself, namely in the part of change management. Researchers come to the conclusion that the success of ERP implementation projects go hand in hand with the focus on change management. Among those surveyed, 72% indicated that ERP implementation projects are increasing focus on managing organizational change. At the same time, investing in change management is extremely low (54 percent of our respondents allocated 25 percent or less of their budget).

Budget cuts can look nice on paper but have catastrophic consequences in the long run. Organizations need to understand where it makes sense to pragmatically minimize costs without minimizing the results.

Failures in implementation projects from a week to six months or more are interrelated with the level of focus on change management and willingness to change. Data suggest that many organizations do not take timely action to reduce risks associated not only with the technical part but also with the ability of people to adapt to change. At the same time, it should be noted that technical failures are characterized by a shorter period of failure and are more easily solved than those related to the human factor. Not only productivity growth but even the very possibility of successful implementation largely depends on the reaction of the personnel of the enterprise, which is both the object and the subject of the transformations.

Management of changes in the implementation of ERP-systems

It is difficult to define and rationalize the importance of managing organizational changes when implementing automated control systems. However, the annual Panorama-Consulting reports show the positive impact of change management on the organization's performance (in the absence of change management when implementing ERP, the performance is low). For example, the report in 2010 shows that (Koh, Gunasekaran & Goodman 2011):

• More than 40% of organizations, along with automation of the management system, carry out other transformations. At least 40% of companies implementing ERP software change the CEO, create new jobs. 26% conduct mergers or acquisitions along with the deployment of the ERP system, 19% - make reductions. The size of such changes makes the implementation of a strong organizational change management program in connection with the implementation of the ERP system even more important.

• People adapt poorly to changes. More than 53% of organizations that implement automated systems evaluate their own ability to cope with changes as pretty bad or very bad. 47% argue that the connection between management and employees leaves much to be desired. Such conditions do not facilitate the effective implementation of ERP. Strategies and tactics of managing organizational changes help to manage organizational risks and overcome resistance to change.

• More than 60% of organizations suffer from not seeing utility in innovation, and the old system does not integrate well with innovation. Consequently, employees using the new

ERP system resist and, and the learning curve requires a long period of time. 62% hardly use new forms of reports and key operational data. Such indicators emphasize the magnitude of the changes that occur as a result of the introduction. An effective organizational change management plan is critical and can help employees understand and use the improvements of the new system.

• Organizations expect a lot from ERP-systems. Companies expect that their corporate software systems contribute to the achievement of business goals. 69% of companies are confident that the systems are implemented to increase business efficiency, 39% hope for standardization of business operations and 39% expect that the work of employees will be facilitated. However, experience and research shows that such expectations are not justified without effective change management.

• Most companies are not ready to implement ERP-systems. They do not involve employees, do not take advantage of process management and other advantages of enterprise software. Almost 50% of organizations in the process of implementing software do not have plans for organizational changes, training or communications. In addition, 42% did not develop implementation evaluation indicators and do not understand the benefits they expect. At this, all this should be realized before the introduction of an automated control system. Otherwise, the organization will not have anything good in result.

Organizational change management is one of the main reasons why companies have succeeded in their ERP initiatives, while the lack of change management plans is the cause of most failures. Success or failure has very little to do with software, so organizations need to carefully plan and allocate resources, taking into account organizational change management activities in the framework of software implementation projects.

Practice confirms that underestimating the influence of the human factor, and, consequently, the lack of special work with personnel during the implementation of ERP, can jeopardize the project's implementation and the welfare of the enterprise as a whole.

According to C. Holland and B.Light (2009), among the main risks, experts identify the

following: the failure to complete the project (i.e., the investment is "wasted"), the departure

of competent employees from the company, the refusal of the IT specialists to introduce or

support a new system, the sabotage of the rank employees.

Thus, projects for the implementation of ERP-systems in enterprises are associated

with significant problems of change management. Underestimation of the importance of the

human factor can provoke a prolongation of the IT implementation process, cause major

economic losses, and in the worst case lead to the failure of the project.

People do not like change, and the introduction of IT, in particular information

systems (IP), requires them to restructure (Hanafizadeh & Ravasan 2011a). In general, the

origins of the problem of personnel resistance in the implementation of IT lie in human

nature, and not in IT (Ovidiu & Dascalu 2010). Resistance to change is an inherent property

of human nature but it can be minimized if the goals of the project coincide with the goals of

the majority of people participating in it.

Often, enterprises are confronted with the so-called "Italian strike," which consists in

the extremely strict performance of employees of the company of their job duties and rules,

not a single step away from them and not a single step beyond them. Sometimes an Italian

strike is called 'work-to-rule.' Employees follow the new rules but only formally, since they

do not see any sense in the ongoing reforms. This method of strike action is very effective,

because it is almost impossible to work strictly according to instructions, because it is

impossible to take into account all the nuances of production activity in them. This form of

protest leads to a significant decline in productivity and, accordingly, to large losses for the

enterprise. Thus, the "Italian strike" of employees regarding the implemented IS leads to a

loss of the meaning of its implementation (Aladwani 2011). For example, the system is present, but does not work or functions incorrectly, and aggregated data, rising to the upper level of the leadership, can distort the real state of affairs.

The opposition of personnel and IS is a wrong approach to the existing problem. IS should be a reflection of the needs of staff and management. Successfully implemented IS is almost always a trade-off between the demands of all its customers and the capabilities of developers.

The introduction of IS in enterprises, as a rule, involves the implementation of a large amount of work with the participation of its employees. Violation of the implementation technology, the complexity of interaction arising within the enterprise, as well as working with implementation consultants lead to the fact that the staff begins to resist the changes.

Negative behavior of personnel in the implementation of IS can be dictated by a lack of understanding of the full implementation process, inadequate knowledge of the tasks that do not take into account the requirements and limitations of the IS functionality.

The transformation of the employees of the enterprise where IS into uninterested observers and the responsibility for the project only by the developer is a situation in which the project of implementation is almost one hundred percent doomed to failure. In this case, there is no systematic vision of the project, a correct understanding of the role of consultants. The management of the enterprise believes that all consultants should implement everything without the participation of employees of the enterprise. As a result, the employees of the ERP provider are turning into operators in the enterprise. Very often, the desire to shorten the time period turns out that future performers are completely eliminated from the project. As a result, the personnel of the enterprise is not ready to work independently at the stage of project delivery. The lack of a common language between the implementation consultants and the management of the enterprise leads to an unpredictable result and, as a result, to the resistance of the personnel of the enterprise to the changes that are being made.

Very often, enterprise managers do not assess how well their staff is ready to implement IS. Employees are frightened by the fact that they will have to learn a huge amount of new information. The consequence of this fear is a negative attitude towards the implemented system (Umble & Umble 2012).

Resistance to change is the result of the fact that end users of new systems do not understand their necessity. In this case, the role of the change support group is to link the goals of management and organization with the interests and understanding of employees.

Support for change at any level directly depends on the level of knowledge and understanding of goals and objectives. Organizations should help each member of the company realize the benefits of the upcoming changes. Since ERP implementation projects are IT-related, the support of these departments is high, and among other seemingly interested parties, as a rule, it is low.

Our survey showed that the increase in terms of implementation in 38% of cases, according to respondents is due to resistance. In most cases, the project team adheres to the rule 'Set a schedule that is both aggressive but realistic. We all know that is easier to say than to do.' However, in its observance, the emphasis is made on the technical component. The lack of communication and learning about change processes is a serious cause of problems. Ideally, communications and training should begin long before implementation. For example, it can be done trough determining the preparedness and communication strategy.

Underestimation of the role of change management and lack of resources to support the management of organizational change has a negative impact on the success of the project. Ultimately, organizations understand that they need to expand the scope of the project budget, but by that time it is already difficult to obtain additional funding.

The formation of an efficiently working ERP implementation team at the enterprise is very important for the success of the automation project. When implementing ERP, the tasks of communication and joint work of representatives of various departments of the enterprise acquire great importance. Implementation of the system is carried out by a team, which, as a rule, includes a coordinating committee (consisting of people who are vitally interested in the success of the project and who have significant influence in the enterprise, but because of objective reasons do not have enough time for direct participation in the work on it), the head of the implementation group (the main person providing the "physical" promotion of the project is the main intermediary between the enterprise and the representatives of the supplier of the system or the consulting firm, if they are involved in the project) and directly the implementation team (on it there is the main workload for the implementation of works related to the implementation of IS in the whole enterprise; when it is formed, it is necessary to ensure that representatives of all enterprise services affected by the introduction are included in its structure) (Aladwani 2011). All members of the implementation team must coordinate their actions with each other, which will result in a well-balanced implementation project.

Motivation is a key element of management, so it is necessary to consider carefully the motivation scheme of the project executors. Not necessarily this should be a big bonus for the successful implementation of the system.

More often than not, the introduction of a new management system helps to increase the status of participants in this work, increases their professional level. These are very significant incentives. For the leader, who forms the "project team", it is important to correctly understand the expectations of the performers related to the success of this case. This can be career growth, increasing wages, gaining new knowledge, reaching new heights in professional growth.

Success is possible only in case of strong support of the project by the company's top management. The introduction of a new management system implies not only the installation of programs for jobs. Such projects are connected with the change of working and managerial processes, redistribution of responsibility and authority. These changes often come into conflict with the interests of those or other heads of departments and employees. As a result, sabotage or open resistance to change begins. Therefore, the head of the organization should openly and clearly support the project team and the results of its work.

The whole scope of works within the project implementation should be divided into separate, independent stages, fixing the expected result and the time of its achievement for each of these stages. One can proceed to the next stage only after fulfilling three conditions:

▪ The project team has developed a unified understanding of the results of the phase;

▪ This understanding is documented;

▪ The results of the stage are accepted by the customer, that is, the enterprise manager.

This approach allows controlling the risks of the project, moving forward to the intended goal. In the course of the project after the completion of the next stage, it is necessary to return to the original objectives of the project and, if necessary, adjust them depending on the changed fundamental requirements, a new vision of the company's development strategy and other factors of impact. The goals and requirements tend to change, and in this regard, the necessary and timely adjustment will allow at the appropriate stage of the project to choose the right direction for subsequent actions within the project.

Researchers emphasize the relationship of investments in ERP with investments in staff training and organizational structure improvement (Abugabah & Sanzogni 2010, Azevedo et al., 2012). IT themselves does not give much. To become more effective than others, it is not enough to buy IT products; one have to introduce them with the mind. American journalist Nicholas Carr in his book (Carr 2003) argues that even new ERP-systems no longer guarantee the company a competitive advantage. ERP is becoming a core technology. They are certainly necessary but strategically meaningless, since the best business practices implemented in ERP systems can be bought and used by any enterprise. Thus, the human factor is becoming increasingly important in the organization of successful IT deployments.

The introduction of a management automation system, like any serious transformation in an enterprise, is a complex and often painful process. However, the positive effect of being competent and successful in various aspects of implementation undoubtedly justifies the resources and efforts aimed at achieving it.

Conclusion

The introduction of modern management solutions brings companies many different business advantages that quickly justify investing resources in projects. However, to achieve the expected results, the project team should properly work on drawing up the project implementation plan, including fixing the key performance indicators of the project (KPI), and very carefully monitor the implementation.

At the moment, the market offers a wide variety of ERP-systems but all systems have the following common characteristics: integration of almost all business processes; a single interface for all users; a single database with permanent access; full software with the ability to flexibly customize for the business processes of a particular company. In general, the implementation of the ERP-system in the company makes it possible to increase the efficiency of its activities. This concerns cross-functional processes that require the consolidation of data from several divisions of the company. ERP-system allows using the most effective methods of work, as at its creation the experience of many companies is used, that have implemented this product and constantly improving product modules in accordance with changing market conditions.

With the help of ERP-systems it is possible to provide interaction both between departments within the company and with external partners. Inside the company, this interaction allows building accountability, using the input data of all company departments without exception, and monitor the company's dynamics online. Interaction with counterparties, the exchange of open information on certain areas of the company's activities reduces the time required for concluding additional agreements and billing. This leads to the tracking of the data of interest by the counteragents themselves who are interested in working with the company in the field of supplying goods and/or providing services within a specified time.

The company that implemented the ERP-system becomes more open, the trust of shareholders and investors increases. These facts have a positive effect on the dynamics of the value of shares, thereby increasing the capitalization of the company.

However, as is known, the quality and efficiency of the system is determined not only by the set of possible functions that this system is capable of performing and implementing, but also by the flexibility of the system, its adaptability to existing processes in the company. When implementing the ERP-system, on the one hand, it is analyzed by the company's management, an assessment of its capabilities is carried out, and on the other - an analysis of the current business processes by the developer of the ERP system. As a result, some kind of third, intermediate system should be obtained, taking into account the peculiarities of the company's functioning.

When deciding on the implementation of ERP, it is very important that the company not only analyzes the functional and technological advantages that the ERP system provides for the company but also compares these advantages with the requirements of the company's strategic development. The task of calculating possible losses from the non-implementation of the ERP introduction project is reduced to calculating losses from not reaching strategic and/or tactical business plans of the company.

The return on investment in the ERP system is not from the system itself but from improving the efficiency of business processes, which it supports. By itself, the enterprise resource management system, no matter how good it is, has a weak impact on increasing the company's productivity. If the company continues to follow the previous business processes after the introduction of the new system, it can expect only the same, or most likely, the worst performance. ERP system can provide and support many new types of processes but it is the company's task to decide what these business processes should be and decide on their subsequent use or rejection. The effectiveness of using the system, which should be calculated to obtain the cost-effectiveness indicator, depends, first of all, on the implementation of a successful business strategy. It is impossible to talk about the correct and effective implementation of information technologies and ERP in particular designed to fundamentally improve the company's market position, without considering the achievement of a certain level of key performance indicators of the company. The system should be 'tuned' to achieve the strategic and tactical goals of the organization. If the companies ignore the corporate strategy when implementing the ERP system and consider its use as a technology for the implementation of exclusively tactical tasks, then, in spite of the indisputable benefits obtained, there may be no fundamental improvements in the company's business. Comparative benefits in such projects are often so small that many people start to regard modern ERP systems as unnecessarily expensive thing. Thus, the utility of the system is significantly reduced, which is critical even at a relatively low total cost of its ownership. Defining the company's business strategy and reflecting this strategy on the goals and objectives that the chosen ERP system is designed to solve is the most important thing in making a decision about implementation.

It should be noted that in some cases there are processes with which ERP-systems do not work, therefore additional software products can work in parallel. In this case, it is necessary to make the programs secondary to the ERP-system, providing for the exchange of data between the system and the programs.

When implementing the ERP-system, one should remember about the possible resistance to changes on the part of employees. The problem is that many projects tend to focus on teaching users how to use the new information system. This is important, but it is necessary to learn to understand how key business processes will depend on ERP, use different training tools (online help, refresher courses, etc.) that are available after the end of the implementation project.

The more employees will be involved in decisions regarding the development and implementation of ERP, the more they will be interested in the project. The more they know about the reasons for choosing ERP, how this will benefit the company, and what this means for performing specific jobs, the less likely resist resistance to change will occur.

The main problem from which many other problems connected the introduction of ERP systems stem is that the implementation of the ERP system is not just an issue of information technology, but rather the management and restructuring of the company's structure. The system cannot be implemented in an enterprise where business processes are not adjusted.

To avoid negative consequences, it is necessary to carefully plan the implementation of changes, promptly identify the causes and sources of resistance, and learn how to overcome them.

One of the main problems of the unsuccessful introduction of changes is the mentality of workers, their potential for resistance to change, novelty. After all, it is quite obvious that organizational change entails the need to abandon the existing behavior, reassess the criteria and structure of governance, and this, as a rule, affects people's interests, which causes their resistance.

To successfully implement the change program, one must define "agents" or "conductors" of the changes. "Change agent" should be an employee of the company, who is free to understand the problems and ways to eliminate them. He should ensure the following:

• Clearly define goals and formulate tasks;

• Be able to adapt goals and objectives to changes;

• Have the skills to form a team and involve representatives of key stakeholder groups in its work;

• Tolerate the state of temporary uncertainty;

• Be able to assess the prospects and results of the implementation of changes.

Potential "agents of change" can be members of the working group on organizational development and members of the working groups in the areas of activity, where changes are planned.

To overcome the resistance of employees, it is necessary to analyze their behavior - to determine their attitude to changes, to identify in advance the reasons for possible resistance.

To overcome resistance, it is recommended to conduct training of personnel, which will equip it with understanding of the need for changes. However, we should not exclude from the learning process any groups of employees. Involvement of the maximum number of employees in the process of change increases the sense of responsibility of each for the implementation of the necessary activities and turns them into active supporters.

In general, when an ERP system is implemented, an enterprise of any size and activity profile receives the following main advantages:

- There is an opportunity to make more informed and operational decisions.

- The number of personnel errors in the enterprise and unnecessary operations is reduced by combining corporate information in a single repository.

- The productivity of the personnel of the enterprise increases.

- Improved quality of customer service and relationships with suppliers, as well as increasing opportunities to increase the number of customers and suppliers.

- Standardized and unified production processes (for example, accounting and control methods), as well as personnel management.

- Improved the ability to forecast and plan the activities of the enterprise (in particular, procurement of materials), which increases the efficiency of the entire production process.

- The time-to-market for new products and services (timetomarket) is shortened due to optimization of business processes and production operations (for example, reduction of order processing time) and the possibility of creating products within IIS (in integration with CAD/CAM/CAE, PDM, etc.).

- Costs for management, not productive expenses and the cost price of production are reduced. At the same time, it should be borne in mind that each module of ERP-system reduces the cost of the corresponding type of management activity, but not the cost of materials, labor, energy, and components. That is, in the cost of the product, the share introduced by the costs of providing management processes is reduced, thereby reducing the cost of the product as a whole.

- There are improved abilities to manage working capital due to a significant reduction in inventory, and, consequently, the turnover of goods and income of the enterprise increase.

To assess the effectiveness of investing in the ERP, a multi-criteria and multi-purpose approach based on the ranking of goals and the ordering of parameters by the hierarchy analysis method may be appropriate.

Reference list

Abugabah, A. & Sanzogni, L. 2010, 'Enterprise Resource Planning (ERP) System in Higher Education: A literature Review and Implications,' *International Journal of Human and Social Sciences*, 5(6), pp. 395-399.

Aladwani, A.M. 2011, 'Change management strategies for successful ERP implementation,' Business Process Management Journal, No 7. Iss. 3, pp. 266 -275.

Allied Market Research official website. Available at:

https://www.alliedmarketresearch.com/

Azevedo, P.S. et al. 2012, 'Advantages, Limitations, and Solutions in the Use of ERP Systems (Enterprise Resource Planning) – A Case Study in the Hospitality Industry,' *Procedia Technology*, 5, pp. 264-272.

Bajwa, D. Garcia, J. & Mooney, T. 2004, 'An integrative framework for the assimilation of enterprise resource planning systems: Phases, antecedents, and outcomes,' *Journal of Computer Information Systems*, Vol. 44, No. 3, pp. 81-90.

Bazhair, A. & Sandhu, K. 2015, 'Factors for the Acceptance of Enterprise Resource Planning (ERP) Systems and Financial Performance,' *J. Econ. Bus. Manag.*, 3, pp. 1–10.

Boston Consulting Group, 2016, BCG Technology Advantages, *October Report.*

Behesti, H. 2006, 'What managers should know about ERP/ERP II,' *Management Research News,* 29(4), pp. 184-193.

Carr, N. 2003, 'IT Doesn't Matter,' *Harvard Business Review*, May, pp 41-49.

Coyne, L., Tiberiu Hajas, Magnus Hallback, Lindstorm, M. and Vollmar, C. 2016, *IBM Private, Public and Hybrid Cloud Storage Solutions*, U.S: IBM.

Creswell, J. 2009, *Research design: Qualitative, quantitative, and mixed methods approaches*, Thousand Oaks, CA: Sage Publications.

Davenport, T. 1990, *The industrial engineering: Information technology and business process redesign*, Massachusetts Institute of Technology.

Dillard, J. F. & Yuthas, K. 2006, 'Enterprise resource planning systems and communicative action,' *Critical Perspectives on Accounting*, Vol. 17, No. 2, pp. 202-223.

Eden, R., Sedera, D. & Tan, F. 2014, 'Sustaining the Momentum: Archival Analysis of Enterprise Resource Planning Systems (2006–2012),' *Commun. Assoc. Inf. Syst.*, 35, pp. 39–82.

Fisher, M. 2006, *Staff perceptions of an enterprise resource planning system implementation: A case study of three Australian universities*. Queensland Central Queensland University. PhD.

Gattiker, T. & Goodhue, D. 2005, 'What Happens After ERP Implementation: Understanding the Impact of Inter-Dependence and Differentiation on Plant-Level Outcomes,' *MIS Quarterly*6 No 29 (3), pp. 559–585.

Grant, G. 2003*, ERP & data warehousing in organizations: Issues and challenge*, Hershey, PA: IRM Press.

Gupta, J., ed. 2009, *Handbook of research on enterprise systems*, New York: Information Science Reference.

Haddara, M. & Zach, O. 2012, 'ERP systems in SMEs: An extended literature review,' *Int. J. Inf. Sci.*, 2, pp. 106–116.

Hanafizadeh, P. & Ravasan, A.Z. 2011a, 'Life after ERP implementation,' *International Journal of Enterprise Information Systems*, No 7, Iss.4, pp. 23-63.

Hanafizadeh, P., & Ravasan, A. Z. 2011b, 'A McKinsey 7S model-based framework for ERP readiness assessment,' *International Journal of Enterprise Information Systems*, No 8, Issue 4, p. 23.

Hardwood, S. 2003, ERP: The implementation cycle. Oxford: Butterworth & Heinemann.

Holland, C. & Light, B. 2009, 'A Critical Success Factors Model for ERP Implementation,' *IEEE Software*, No 05/6, pp. 30–35.

Huang S., Chang, I., Li, S. & Lin, M. 2005, 'Assessing risk in ERP projects: Identify and prioritize the factors,' *Industrial Management & Data Systems*, 104(8), pp. 681-688.

Ilfinedo, P., & Nahar, N. 2006, Prioritization of Enterprise Resource Planning (ERP) systems success measures: Viewpoints of two organizational stakeholder groups. *Proceedings of the 2006 ACM symposium on Applied computing, April 23-27, 2006. Dijon, France*, pp. 1554-1560.

Kim, Y., Lee, Z., & Gosain, S. 2005, 'Impediments to successful ERP implementation process,' *Bus. Process. Manag. J.* 11, pp. 158-170.

Koh, S.L., Gunasekaran, A. & Goodman, T. 2011, 'Drivers, barriers, and critical success factors for ERPII implementation in supply chains: A critical analysis,' *The Journal of Strategic Information Systems*, Vol. 20, No. 4, pp. 385-402.

Laukkanen, S., Sarpola, S. & Hallikainen, P. 2007, 'Enterprise Size Matters: Objectives and Constraints of ERP Adoption,' *J. Enterp. Inf. Manag.*, 20, pp. 319–334.

Law, C. & Ngai, E. 2007, 'An investigation of the relationships between organizational factors, business process improvement and ERP success,' *Benchmarking: Int. J.* 14, pp. 387–406.

Lenart, A. 2011, ERP in the Cloud – Benefits and Challenges. In: Wrycza S. (eds) Research in Systems Analysis and Design: Models and Methods. SIGSAND/PLAIS 2011. Lecture Notes in Business Information Processing, Vol. 93. Springer, Berlin, Heidelberg.

Maditinos, D., Chatzoudes, D. & Tsairidis, C. 2011, 'Factors affecting ERP system implementation effectiveness,' *J. Enterp. Inf. Manag.*, 25, pp. 60–78.

Muscatello, J., & Chen, I. 2008, 'Enterprise Resource Planning (ERP) Implementations: Theory and Practice,' *International Journal of Enterprise Information Systems*, Vol.4, No. 1, pp. 63-83.

Ovidiu, S. & Dascalu, C. 2010, 'The Advantages and Risks of Using an ERP System in the Context Globalization,' *International Journal of Modern Manufacturing Technologies*, Vol. II, Iss. 2, pp. 83-88.

Peng, G. & Gala, C. 2014, 'Cloud ERP: A new dilemma to modern organisations?' *J. Comput. Inf. Syst.*, 54, pp. 22–30.

Scheer, A.W. & Habermann, F. 2010, 'Enterprise resource planning: making ERP a success', *Communications of the ACM*, No 43, Iss.4, pp. 57–61.

Soja, P. 2008, 'Examining the conditions of ERP implementations: Lessons learnt from adopters,' *Bus. Process. Manag. J.* 14, pp. 105-123.

Soliman, M. & Karia, N. 2016, 'Enterprise Resource Planning (ERP) Systems in the Egyptian Higher Education Institutions: Benefits, Challenges and Issues,' *Proceedings of the 2016 International Conference on Industrial Engineering and Operations Management Kuala Lumpur, Malaysia,* March 8-10, 2016.

Tingting, H. & Yasuda, R. 2016, 'Comprehensive review of literature survey articles on ERP,' Business Process Management Journal, No 22. Iss. 1, pp. 2-32.

Tortorella, G.L. & Fries, C.E. 2015, Reasons for adopting an ERP system in a public University in Southern Brazil, *Proceedings of the 2015 International Conference on Operations Excellence and Service Engineering Orlando, Florida, USA, September 10-11, 2015.*

Ugrin, J. 2009, 'The effect of system characteristics, stage of adoption, and experience on institutional explanations for ERP systems choice,' *Accounting Horizons*, vol. 23, no. 4, pp. 365-389.

78

Umble, E. & Umble, M. 2012, 'Avoiding ERP implementation failure,' *Industrial Management*, vol. 44, no. 1, pp. 25-33.

Vaman, J. 2007, *ERP in practice: ERP strategies for steering organizational competence and competitive advantage*, New Delhi: Tata McGraw-Hill Publishing Company.

van Vuuren, I.J. & Seymour, L.F. 2013, '*Towards a model for user adoption of enterprise systems in SMEs*,' Enterprise Systems Conference (ES), Cape Town, pp. 1-9.

Venkatraman, S. & Fahd, K. 2016, 'Challenges and Success Factors of ERP Systems in Australian SMEs,' *Systems*, Vol.4, Iss. 20, pp. 1-18.

Yongbeom, K. Zoonky, L. & Gosain, S. 2015, 'Impediments to successful ERP implementation process,' Business Process Management Journal, No 11. Iss. 2. pp. 158–170.

Zhong, F. & Rohde, M.E. 2014, Cloud Computing and ERP: A Framework of Promises and Challenges, *25th Australasian Conference on Information Systems 8th -10th Dec 2014, Auckland, New Zealand.*